ROBERT L. VOGT

The
Death
of a
Wife

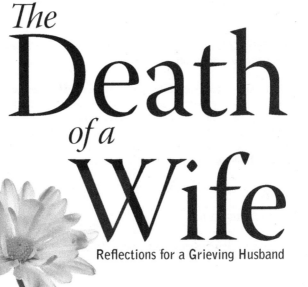

Reflections for a Grieving Husband

acta
PUBLICATIONS

The Death of a Wife
Reflections for a Grieving Husband
Robert L. Vogt

Editing: Gregory F. Augustine Pierce

Cover image: Shutterstock.com
Cover and book design: Tau Publishing Design Department

Published by ACTA Publications, 4848 N. Clark Street, Chicago, IL 60640, (800) 397-2282, www.actapublications.

Library of Congress Number: 96-084025

ISBN: 978-0-87946-141-6

Printed in the United States of America by Total Printing Systems

Second Edition

Year 30 29 28 27 26 25 24 23 22 21 20 19 18

Printing 15 14 13 12 11 10 9 8 7 6 5

acta
PUBLICATIONS

Contents

To Fran

Foreword

We have been told by both the very learned and the sadly experienced that in order to heal after the death of a loved one, we must first struggle through a journey of grief.

Acknowledging our loss, working through the emotional pain, adjusting to a life that no longer includes our loved one or the roles that were so uniquely his or hers, and beginning to reinvest our energy in order to gather our memories are all part of a wrenching process with which all who mourn are faced.

We each find our own way to travel on this journey, but the struggle eludes no one. Some people go to support groups, many find a trusted friend or counselor to talk to. Some spend endless hours in reading; others choose to pour out their thoughts on paper, hoping that by expressing their grief in the written word they can come to understand what they are going through.

The author of *The Death of a Wife* has found God on his personal journey through grief. The discovery does not come easily; it torments him. But the struggle permeates his stories and is weaved through his poetry until he can finally let go and say "good-bye" to his beloved wife.

It is my hope that those husbands who grieve the death of a spouse will find in these beautiful reflections an assurance that though they grieve, now they can, as the author has, work through their grief and move on with their lives. Perhaps, as he has, they will discover that their God will walk that journey of sadness with them.

—Mauryeen A. O'Brien, O.P., Author, *New Day Journal*

Seasons of Love

We met in springtime.
Our every meeting, word, touch or phone call
warm, new, exciting
Every sense alive with the birth of us.
The season of spring love
filled with hope
and expectancy.

We married in summer.
The season of married love
hot with passion
sweaty with plans
of house
job
children.

Our love matured in fall.
The season of fall love
quiet
knowing the reality of each other
with the leafy colors of our lives shining bright
in the cool, delightful
fall season
of love.

It is now the winter of our love.
Your death wraps its icy fingers around us
our love hurries into hibernation
awaiting a new spring of resurrected life.
The season of winter love is hard
harsh
numb fingers feel so little
hat-ed, coat-ed body numb.

The Something

Something disappeared. It just went away. One second it was here, the next, gone. The here and the gone were worlds apart, as far apart as anything I had ever experienced—like "Yes" and "No"; cold and hot; wet and dry.

That day started badly.

Unconsciousness had set in. Breathing was labored. The need for morphine frequent. The day passed slowly as thrashing started and increased. Then breathing slowed, became intermittent, one breath every moment or so—deep and long. Then nothing. Waiting. Hoping. But no more. That's when the Something disappeared.

Clothes still there. Body still there. Oxygen tanks still there. Books and papers still there. Rosary and scapulars still there. The bed was still there, but Something was gone. The Something's going killed the clothes, the medicine, the body, the books, the rosary and the scapulars. Oh, they were still there, but they were dead, because the Something was gone. The Something's going destroyed, totally annihilated, so much.

When I was little, I used to play ball in a school yard near my house. For hours, I would bounce a tennis ball against a brick wall. I threw that ball against the wall and the ball would come back to me.

The solid, brick wall created a relationship between me and playing ball. I depended on the wall, for a necessary part of the game was the wall. Then one day I went to play ball in the school yard and the wall was gone—they tore it down to make more parking space. I remember standing where the wall had been— lost, sad, knowing the game was over. I felt that if I threw the ball it would go forever, for my ball playing world now had no boundary.

So when the Something left, I felt I had no boundaries—like living in a house with no walls. The Something had provided stability. Against it I threw what I was and it came bouncing back—husband, friend, lover, companion. But no more, for when the Something disappeared, came tumbling down, who I was floated out into endless space.

Last fall, while raking leaves, I lost my lighter. It just fell out of my pocket, mingling with and lost in the leaves. But its going was singular. All that was gone was a lighter. It didn't take anything with it. Several times I have lost keys, a pen, a quarter. Each of these goings was insignificant, influencing and affecting limited spheres of my life. But when the Something left, It reverberated through my whole life. It rolled and tumbled through every emotion. Reaching out and slapping work, prayer, church, finances, even family structure.

When I lost keys, a lighter, a pen, a playground wall or some change, I accepted the loss. I believed they were gone. But when the Something disappeared, it was impossible to believe It was gone. I couldn't even force myself to believe it. Each attempt at belief brought waves of nausea.

Once, too, I lost a baseball. I hit it into Miss Taylor's flower patch and just left it there. Nobody messed with Miss Taylor's flowers! No one ever dared rummage through her flower bed even to find a lost ball. So the baseball was gone, there was a finality about its going. But not like the finality of the Something's going. With the Something's going, I realized finality is a continuum, with the finality of the Something's going way out on the extreme end. This finality takes your breath away, like a sniff of ammonia. You can get another baseball, another pen, another quarter or even another wall, but not another Something. Once gone, it's gone forever.

When you lose a lighter, a pen, a baseball, you can describe what is lost. You can describe its size, shape, weight and color. But when you lose your wife's Something, you stand steeped in stupidity. For the Something that is gone has no shape, no color, no size. You can't see, feel, taste or smell It. You can't describe It. You just know It was there and now is gone. It animated, It enlivened all the trappings of daily existence. It was a fire that warmed each moment. The coldness of each moment now tells you It is gone. Knowing by absence is terrible knowledge.

When the Something of a wife and lover and friend goes, you search for It everywhere and often. Sex, booze, TV, work, all beckon, "Here It is." But, of course, It isn't. The frustration, the anger, the guilt, the self-pity of the Something's going are resolved and washed away only in tears. The Something's disappearance teaches that it really isn't that hard for a man to cry.

The pain of the going of the Something of a loved one rubs your insides raw, and the open rawness exposes you to others and their pain. Each newspaper obituary is a sharp slap in the face. Each funeral home visit is walking over the sharp piercing glass of another's pain. Their pain enters you. You know with them, you suffer with them. You enter their grieving presence with compassion. Somehow their pain and your pain is ours— not mine, not yours—just ours.

As you realize the Something is gone, you limp into prayer, mouthing, "Thy will be done. You know what is best." Yet as you say the words, you know you are a coward, afraid to express your honest anger; afraid to wish God into the depths of hell for letting this happen. You hear your real, quiet, still voice behind the "Thy will be done," as "Damn You!" punctuates petitions of the Our Father.

Your prayer is hurt, anger, frustration, wondering about and questioning the goodness of God's will. Often prayer is no more than the constant repetition of, "Your ways are not my ways; Your thoughts are not my thoughts." It seems you never accept the Something's going as the will of God; it is too devastating to see death as something willed. So you approach God's providence from views of a different kind of justice, a different system of values, a different set of rewards—His ways, His thoughts; definitely not my thoughts or ways.

You sit numbed with the Something's remains. Clothes, jewelry, favorite cup, special chair, oils and lotions and body. You then learn reality. What is real is what is gone. What is illusion is what remains. What is real is not seen. What is illusion is visible. The whole experience changes your values. Muscle tone, trim waist, wavy hair, money, reputation—are these real or illusion? Car, house, bank account, job, manicured lawn—real, illusion?

The Something's going forces you to search for, be aware of, and experience the Something of others. You look for that Something of men and women, that Something of plants and animals, that Something of self. What is that Something? Where is that Something? How do you get a handle on that Something? As you search, you notice a lot of illusion, a lot of excessive baggage in your life and in your relationships.

Then, one day, in time, the Something begins to return.

It comes slowly, vaguely. The Something fades in and out in the mist of prayer, the time after Communion. You feel the Something in the acceptance of an Offertory as you mix your special water with the wine and the Something is present in the "Yes" of each Morning Offering. In all of these you sense the Something, present, alive, caring, so different, yet so real. You reach out in freedom to embrace the Something. Not the tingling of the former naked, skin to skin embrace, just a calm, quiet, powerful, "it's-okay" embrace, that squeezes from your very depths, "Eternal rest grant unto her, O Lord."

The wonder, the greatness of the Something's vague return is in that "okay." The loss, the hurt, the pain, the why, remain. The loneliness, the separation, the quiet, still stalk like a hungry bear. Laughing couples holding hands, families crunching fries at McDonald's, mothers shopping with their daughters—all still hit like a January wind. But, finally, it's okay. The vague, present, quiet Something walks with you and flavors your world, and you pray, "Eternal rest, O Lord, to both of us."

Finally, without tears, without self-destruction, without anger, without hopelessness, you realize that the Something is home. Her journey is finished. You see her hand reaching out to secure your own journey home. In her safe journey home and in the hand securing your own journey home, you see the faint glimmer of an answer to that ever-present question, "Why? O, my God, why?"

What I Need

Friends
    eyes averted
    hands in pockets
Ask what I need.

What I need is
    a little drink
    a piece of bread
    and a place at your table.

People
    words stumbling
    tears choked
    feet shuffling
Ask what they can do.

What I need is
    a little drink
    a piece of bread
    and a place at your table.

You can't take the pain away
    don't even try
You can't help me with the
    "Why?"
    please don't try!

Don't tell me
    she is better off
        happier now
    God knows best
    we'll be together someday.
Tomorrow, someday and even God
    don't touch my now.

What I need is
    a little drink
    a piece of bread
    and a place at your table.

Please don't pious cliché
    this death
    this fear
    this hurt.

What I need is
    a little drink
    a piece of bread
    and a place at your table.

Bob's New Clothes

Once upon a time in Cincinnati, Ohio, seven-year-old Bob Cummins walked into his house after a hard day of backyard playing and found a shocking surprise waiting for him. Spread out on his bed was a whole new set of clothing. New shirt. New pants. New cap. New socks. New sneakers. New everything. As Bob looked at all the new clothes, he heard his mother say, "It's time to get rid of your old clothes. It's time for a whole new set of clothing."

Well, Bob about had a fit! He didn't want any new clothes. He wanted his old ones. The old ones were comfortable. He was used to them. He knew them and they knew him. The old clothes fit him. He couldn't imagine being without his old clothes and wondered if his friends would even recognize him in new ones. He thought about all the trouble involved in breaking in a new set of clothing. The new clothes would scratch. They would feel so funny. They would be so stiff and unbending. He really wanted no part of the new clothes.

Bob then started the usual, childish, pleading game. "You can give me back my clothes if you want. You don't have to take my clothes away," he said to his mother. But his mother was adamant. The old clothes had to go and they went with a rigid finality. They were gone, for good.

Bob looked at his mother in shocked dismay. He tried to think of something that he did wrong to make her act this way.

Surely he must have done something very bad for her to do this to him, for her to take away all of his old clothes. But he couldn't think of anything unusually bad that he had done. Of course, he had forgotten to take out the garbage several times, had not always washed behind his ears or flossed his teeth every time he brushed. But there was nothing he could think of that he had done that would make her act this way. He couldn't stop thinking that his mother was punishing him by taking away his old clothes—but he couldn't pinpoint exactly what he had done.

With some anger and a lot of hurt, Bob picked up his new clothes slowly from the bed and even more slowly put them on. Then he went out into the neighborhood with the new clothes on.

To his surprise, his friends were kind and sympathetic. Oh, there were a few jokes abut how "dandy" and "dapper" he looked, some ribbing about how with his new clothes all the girls would be chasing him. But for the most part Bob and his new clothes got understanding looks and comments.

As he moved about the neighborhood, Bob felt, in fact, that people were too kind, kind to the point of unreality. He found that most of his friends could say nothing about his new clothes but inane clichés.

Chubby Millett, for instance, told Bob the old clothes were better off now, sort of at peace after hard wear. That made no sense to Bob. He looked around and saw plenty of clothing still in use that was older and much more worn than his had been.

Bill Jones told him simply, "It's what your mother wanted," but this was just a fact and not an explanation. Bob wanted to know why his mother wanted him to be rid of the old clothes and into the new. Bob wanted explanations, not facts.

Another old friend of his told him that he had lost his old clothes several years ago. His mother did the same thing, just took his clothes away and gave him new ones. This was somewhat comforting to Bob, at least he now knew a fellow sufferer. But having fellow sufferers does not take away the pain of losing old clothes, nor does it relieve the scratchiness of new clothes.

His cousin, Kitty, probably said it best. She told him simply that she just didn't know what to say, but she felt bad for him. Bob liked that. For there are no adequate words for a young boy all decked out in stiff, awkward, scratchy, unfamiliar new clothes after losing his old, familiar, soft clothes.

When Bob returned home right before supper, he went upstairs to his room. He wanted to be alone. In the familiarity of his room, he thought about his old clothes. He remembered the good times: ball games played with the sneakers; cap that shaded the sun from his eyes so often; shirt pulled and tugged at through so many football games and games of "Hide-&-Seek" or "Red Rover." As he remembered each article of old clothing, Bob started to weep. Strangely, he wasn't embarrassed by the tears. He saw the tears and the sadness as a natural part of his life. He was grieving for something that had given him so much pleasure, so much joy, so much meaning and purpose in life. He knew that not to weep would be to deny the joy and beauty of his old clothes.

In time, Bob's new clothes became comfortable. He got used to them and found them useful and helpful. But he never forgot his old clothes, they remain a part of him. They live on in every joy, comfort and happiness that any clothing now gives him.

Caressed Fist

The night you died
    I sat in what used to be our bedroom
    and raised my fist to heaven.
In reply
    moonlight, through the window,
    warm, soft, loving, glowing,
    circled my clenched fist.

At your burial, I raised my fist to heaven
    anger, frustration, despair, hopelessness
    expressed.
In reply
    the sun kissed my bruised fist,
    a soft breeze wrapped lovingly around it.

Weeks after your death
I paused, relived that last breath,
And raised my fist to God.
In reply
    gentle raindrops softened my hardened fist.

Now, each time when your death returns
I still raise my fist to heaven
Not in anger
    but to be loved, comforted and caressed.

God's Will

John Bayley slowly pulled his car into the driveway and just sat there. He was exhausted and dreaded going into the house. He had just finished taking the kids back to college, the trip to the various schools had gone well, better than he had expected. The kids had spent the last week and a half at home, not on vacation but attending to the details and ceremonies of their mother's death and burial.

John looked at the house, knew it was now totally empty. For the first time in years he would walk into a house with no one there—no wife, no children. He dreaded going in, dreaded seeing what he knew was there—the dishes, the pictures, the rugs, the furniture, the emptiness. Each would be a silent reminder of everything he wanted to forget.

He knew he was depressed, let down. The funeral arrangements had been a welcome distraction, but now they were over. His depression went deeper though, beyond his wife's death, beyond the funeral and burial. At the two colleges where he dropped off the kids, someone had said to him, "It's God's will." He found this very depressing, for in no way could he see how his wife's death was God's will. Why would God will this to happen? Maybe God didn't intervene, maybe God just stood by and let his wife die. John could accept this. He didn't want a God jumping around, hopping around from disease to disease, curing everyone He ran across. But "It's God's will" was too much for him. He couldn't understand this, didn't believe it, and as usual thought something was wrong with him because he couldn't believe it.

John finally got out of the car and went into the house. It was worse than he anticipated. Nothing in marriage or in family life prepares you for that first time you enter an empty house after the death of a spouse. When he opened the door and stepped into the living room, it was like someone kicked him hard in the stomach. Waves of nausea gripped his stomach, he stumbled to the couch, gasping for breath, then started weeping. The quiet, the silence, the memories were oppressive and stifling. "So," he thought, "*this* is the will of God!"

As days turned into weeks, weeks into months, John found the house, the quiet, the empty becoming almost tolerable. He still felt his wife's absence, but he was handling it. Her absence, her death, he put away in a drawer in his mind, taking it out only once in a while, briefly turning it over and examining it, then quickly putting it back in the drawer. Over time, he was able to open the drawer more often, and look longer.

But the "will of God" thing still haunted him. Did God really will that his wife die? If so, what kind of God was this? What kind of person would will, would want, would command a slow, painful death? No matter how hard he tried, John could not bring himself to say, or believe, "It's God's will."

As he sat alone at home during long evening hours, he pondered the will of God, pondered it until he realized that it was beyond him. There was no answer. No matter how hard he tried, or what theological or philosophical manipulations he used, he could not believe that God willed his wife's death.

John then started mentally building a case for the loving,

kind, gentle will of God. God, he knew, willed babies and fine summer days; God willed cool, forest breezes and willed that both sex and steak be good and refreshing.

He thought of all the wonderful, magnificent, glorious and happy things that God had willed—soft, baby skin; sunrises and sunsets; the trust of childhood and the wisdom of old age.

Even with these thoughts he still did not believe that God willed the death of his wife. But he did become able to trust that somehow, someway, her death was part of some kind of a plan—a willed plan that was kind and loving.

John realized that this question of the "will of God" and his wife's death could not be taken on directly, could not be approached head-on. So he rested and trusted in a roundabout way, a way that saw the goodness of God's will all around and then trusted that somehow this same goodness was present in his wife's death.

John still finds the empty house oppressive, his wife's absence painful. He still cannot say, "Her death is God's will." But he has come to a certain peace about the will of God. He has come to realize that because God's will is so kind and gentle and loving in so many areas of life and experience, he must trust that somehow death must be part of that will.

This act of trust answers no questions, gives no reasons, provides no explanations. It does, however, allow John and God to live together in peace—enough peace for John to pray often, "Thy will be done, on earth..." Enough peace for John to join another wondering, bewildering death cry, "Father, into Your hands I commend my spirit."

God Sighed

God sighed
    and you,
    a small, quiet puff,
    came forth
To float through the universe.

Once you paused in your flight
    and whirlwind-ed through my life.
Your windy chaos rearranged all of me.

One day when I was inattentive
    God inhaled, you disappeared
    floated back to your origin.

The Special Drop

In a land far, far away there was a river which flowed quietly and peacefully; it was a secure, safe and happy river.

If you looked closely at the river, you could see that it was one wide, united body of water. Oh, there were individual drops of water in the river, but the drops flowed into each other. You could hardly see the multitude of individual drops, so united were they with each other. The drops of water in the river were like a bunch of people hugging each other so closely, so tightly, you could hardly tell them apart.

One day a terrible thing happened to the river. The earth shifted; there was an earthquake and the split in the earth cut right through and across the river. The shifting from the earthquake caused a waterfall to appear in the river.

As the river approached the new waterfall, each drop of water became very afraid. The drops started to separate. The oneness of the river ceased and it became many individual drops instead of one united body of water.

As the individual drops started over the waterfall, they experienced loneliness and separation for the very first time. Each drop forgot about the other drops, pushed them away and thought only about itself. Each drop looked down to the bottom of the waterfall, saw the rocks at the bottom and watched other drops hit the rocks and be destroyed. All of the drops screamed in fear as they fell headlong towards the rocks. Fear, panic, self-protection spread through the once quiet, peaceful and secure river.

The river boiled and churned for many a year with the self protection of each of the drops. Then one day a special drop of water appeared in the river. This special drop was different. She told the other water drops that they had to take care of each other; that despite the fear, anxiety and pain of going over the waterfall, everything would be okay. All they had to do was remember the oneness and security of the river and hold hands as they went over the falls. Some drops laughed at this, others called her names, but some listened.

Soon the special drop came to the waterfall. It was her turn to go over the falls. The drop was very afraid. She screamed in fear and anxiety as she tumbled towards the rocks. Yet, despite the fear, she kept remembering the oneness, the peace and safety the river once had, and the special drop reached out to other drops and held their hands. She told them everything would be okay. Then she hit the rocks below the waterfall.

When the special drop hit the rocks, a very strange thing happened. She felt her life cease, but then she immediately bounced off the rocks and started to flow again.

She started what seemed to be a new river, beyond the waterfall, beyond the rocks. But, although it looked like a new river, it really was a continuation of the old river.

Some of the drops going over the waterfall with the special drop saw what happened. They shouted to each other, "The special drop made it. She was right. We will be okay." They shouted back to drops in the middle of the waterfall, to the ones at the top and to the ones approaching the waterfall, "The special drop made it. She hit the rocks, but she's okay. She told us we would be okay too, and we are."

Today if you visit the river and listen very, very carefully you can hear a murmur. But you have to be very, very quiet to hear it. The murmur in the river is the drops talking to each other, whispering and shouting, "It's going to be okay. The special drop told us so. She made it. So can we. Just hold on to each other. Hold on."

Grave Visits

Why do I keep coming here?
You're not here, I know that well.
Dirt, grass, silence,
    name spelled in raised iron letters
That's not you.

But something draws me.
My need for the see-able, the touch-able,
    the real
Is here somehow satisfied.

Only here in
    this vault
        this space
        this place
Can I voice my pain, my experience.

Here for a while I can find you.
That's why I come here
    again
    and again.

The Plot Changes

Like a newborn infant coming out of the womb, John Williams stepped from the wings onto the stage. The bright lights momentarily blinded him, the stage heat contrasted sharply with the coolness of the wings. John was nervous, this was his first play and in it he had the leading role.

The play in which John had the lead was a fairly simple one, the plot neither complex nor deeply psychological. It was the story of a middle-class husband and wife raising three children in the suburbs of a large American city. There was point and counterpoint between suburban and metropolitan living, contrasting educational, social, environmental and emotional issues arising from the two differing value systems and cultures.

John had practiced hard, knew his lines, trusted the other actors; so he felt comfortable, despite the usual stage-fright jitters. He was especially comfortable with the director, a man with many successful plays to his credit—several of them Broadway hits.

The director always built into each of his plays a variety of props—pictures on walls, plants, animals, floor markings, special lights and even colors—to help the actors remember both action and script. The director even placed various persons—voices, he called them—in the wings around the stage to prompt faltering dialogue or whisper stage movements. Thus John was secure in his role. He knew what to say, what to do and knew if any trouble arose he had the director and his "voices" to fall back on.

The first two acts of the three-act play went well, John thought. His dialogue was smooth and crisp, his movements flowing and precise. The play had gone well through the meeting and eventual marriage of the husband and wife, through childbearing and through the settling in a small suburban town. The conflicts of the second act were well developed, as suburban values clashed with metropolitan values and as the children grew, matured and incorporated city values into their lifestyle, much to the dismay of their parents. As the curtain fell on the second act, John felt good about his performance and looked forward to act three.

The third and last act of the play started with a knock at the front door. John was startled, he didn't remember the script calling for a knock to start the third act. Confused, he walked stage right and opened the door to see a uniformed policeman standing there. "There's no policeman in the third act," John thought to himself.

Slowly, quietly and very deliberately, the policeman told John, "I'm sorry to inform you that your wife was killed this afternoon." Just as slowly, quietly and deliberately the policeman turned away from the door and exited into the wings.

John mechanically closed the door, his hand pressed against his forehead. To the audience it looked like he was in shock from the news about his wife. John was in shock—not from the news but from the fact that act three had no knock at the door, no policeman and no accidental death of his wife. The script for act three—as John had rehearsed it over and over—had him and his wife gracefully growing old together, watching their children and a new generation of grandchildren face the never-ending culture clash between suburbs and large city.

"What's going on?" John asked himself as he stood on the stage without words, without action, without any idea of story line or plot, wondering what he was to do. He then heard the director whisper, "Trust me, follow the cues, the prompts, listen to the voices."

The third act seemed a nightmare to John. He caught snatches of dialogue from the voices as he stumbled around the stage. He listened intently as he moved from place to place on the stage following the direction of the cues and voices. "Cry, it's what you should do... Be confused, it's okay... Stage down, turn right and look like you don't know what to do, lean on the actor entering stage left..." the voices directed him.

It wasn't hard for him to act like he didn't know what to do, for John had no idea what to do. The plot was new, the dialogue was new, all movements were new. The third act was totally ad lib—John following the cues of the director and his voices. He listened and watched as his part in the play developed with props he had never seen before and through snatches of dialogue that came from the various voices from the wings.

Finally the play ended, the curtain fell. When the play ended John didn't wait around for curtain calls but rushed off stage immediately to find the director. He found him smiling and applauding in the wings.

"You changed the whole third act," John sputtered. "It was totally different from what we rehearsed. You changed the plot while I was on stage, you didn't warn me, we never rehearsed this."

The director only smiled and told him, "You did great. You handled it well. You're a good actor."

John wasn't in the mood for compliments, he wanted an

explanation. "Why? Why did you do this to me?" he demanded.

With a slight edge of irritation, the director told John, "It's my play. I direct it. I change it as I see fit. Your job is to act, which means you follow my directions."

As his irritation faded, the director explained. "I want actors to stretch and reach to follow the plot," he said. "Anyone can follow action and dialogue that has been rehearsed over and over. The very best acting occurs when an actor puts himself totally in the hands of the director, when the actor's every word and movement flow from the director, not contaminated by the ideas, plans, desires or interpretation of the actor."

Defensively, John asked, "What about the critics?"

"There are no critics," the director answered. "The only critic of my plays is the actor. You and only you critique your performance. Think about it. Which was your best act: one, two or three?"

With that the director walked away, leaving John to his own thoughts. He had to admit that act three was his best, for he did have to stretch himself and reach out and adapt to new words, actions and movements. Never before, he realized, had he really acted like that.

Later, at the cast party, John gained further insight into the methods of the director. He talked to other actors who had also endured surprise plot changes. One had all the stage lights go out during the first act. She performed the rest of the play in total stage darkness. Another, thinking the knock at the door was a delivery of groceries, found his mother standing there needing round-the-clock care from his family. Several others told John of unrehearsed deaths, injuries, divorces and illnesses that were not part of the original plays.

All of them admitted that—despite the confusion, the anger, the initial fright—as long as they followed the prompts and listened to the voices the plot changes made them better, more accomplished actors. They understood and accepted the vital role of the director in their plays, even if they might not have written the surprises in the same way.

Footsteps

Some days I sit in the kitchen
    looking down at the linoleum
    counting the blocks
    following the pattern of circles and squares.
Some days
    it's all I can do
        sit
        stare
        count.

But some days
    from the linoleum
    come sounds
Sounds of your footsteps
        muffled in breakfast slippers
        clicking in dressed up high heels
        rushing from refrigerator to stove to table
        pounding angrily at my lateness for supper
        hurt because I forgot our anniversary
        seductive with all the kids out of the house.

I find you, live with you
    and with my God,
Not in some harp-playing, far-off heaven
    but rather in these linoleum footsteps
    the sounds of our lives together.

Lost in the Department Store

Out of the corner of his eye, six-year-old Will Thompson could see the TV set showing a "Bugs Bunny" videotape. He knew his mother told him to stay right beside her as she looked through various racks of clothing. The music from the videotape, however, was bouncy, the action fast and, after all, it was Bugs. So Will quietly walked away from the adult clothing racks and settled in by the advertising for Looney Toons books, tapes and clothing.

After what seemed to him to be only a few moments, Will grew tired and headed back to his mother. With just a few steps, he realized he had no idea which direction to take. He didn't remember where his mother was. He was lost. His mother was gone.

He started wandering up and down the aisles of the store, but could find his mother nowhere. Several shoppers looked at him and he started to say to them, "I'm lost." He thought better of it, however. He thought he could find his mother on his own. He also figured they should know just by looking at him—a six-year-old little boy alone—that he was lost. Besides, he was ashamed of being lost. He felt being lost was a bad thing, so he didn't want to tell anyone about it.

Will wanted to cry, but felt that, too, was bad. He thought of his dad and his uncles telling him, "Big boys don't cry." So he stiffened his lip and choked back the tears.

As he passed through the automotive section of the store and headed for housewares, Will started to be really afraid. He hadn't been separated from his mother more than a few minutes, but it seemed forever to him. He noticed other small children walking through the store, their hands held securely by their mothers, and he felt acute loneliness.

The store, with all the people milling around in it, seemed so busy to him. No one seemed to care that he was lost, that he couldn't find his way back to his mother. The whole place seemed so unfriendly. "Don't they know I'm lost?" Will thought to himself. "Don't they care?" He longed for someone to take his hand, to tell him that everything was going to be okay, that his mother would soon be found. Yet the people in the store, intent on their various shopping chores, just passed him by.

When he got to the toy section, tears of fear, loneliness and frustration started to form in the corners of his eyes, despite what his dad and uncles had told him.

A heavyset, elderly lady noticed Will standing near the toys. Her own children were all grown men and women now, but she remembered that look—the look her own children had when they were afraid, lonely or lost. She walked over to Will and asked, "Son, are you lost? Is there anything I can do to help you?"

The smile on her face and the kindness in her voice assured Will that she was safe, that she could and would help him.

Will blurted out, "I lost my mommy. I can't find her anywhere."

The woman reached out and gently took Will's hand and started toward the security office—stopping en route only to get Will a pretzel and small Coke.

In no time, Will heard the announcement, "Mrs. Thompson, your son, Will, is at the store security office in the housewares department." Soon he was tearfully reunited with his mother.

Will naturally got a stern lecture about listening and about not wandering off by himself. The sternness, though, was tempered by his mother's evident relief at finding him.

Despite the lecture, Will didn't learn much about listening or wandering off by himself—he would have to get lost several more times before he learned those lessons. He did learn, however, that department stores could be friendly places, that other people could be kind and trusted and helpful. Most of all, he learned that when he was lost he had to tell someone about it, had to admit both to himself and to someone else that he was lost before the process of getting found could start.

Cocoon

This grassy plot
    with marble slab
        noting your name and life span
It is called a grave.

And so it is,
    a place of death.

But this grassy death place
    is a cocoon
    where caterpillar you
    are transformed into that
    someday butterfly.

I kneel in expectation at
    this grassy kaleidoscopic plot
    of death and birth
        joy and sorrow
    from which you will someday fly
        multi-colored
And over spread my all-too-sad life.

Thar She Blows

"Thar she blows! Thar she blows!" shouted the small crowd watching Tony Demling as the oak twig he was holding twitched and then pointed straight down to the ground. They knew they were exaggerating, there was no gusher and never would be one, but the pointing, twitching stick in Tony's hand had found water again.

One of the onlookers, Tim Conley, remarked, "Old T.D. is really good," reflecting the general admiration of the crowd. For the spot in the town where Tony had just found water was rocky, barren and mostly arid. Nobody thought any water could be found where Tony had just found it.

Tony Demling, affectionately referred to as T.D., was a dowser. Had been one all his life. Even as a young boy he had the ability to dowse—to find water by taking a forked twig in his hands, holding it in front of him and then walking through a field until the twig twitched and pointed straight down to where to dig for water.

The people of Lanesville liked T.D., not just because he found places for them to dig wells for water but also because he was a very simple dowser. Some dowsers they knew used fancy dowsing equipment like pendulums or arrowheads with elaborate feathers, and then did their dowsing with complicated ritual-dancing, stomping, hand-waving, head bobbing and complex breathing. T.D., however, used only a forked twig

45

and calmly, simply walked through a field until the stick in his hands found water. The townspeople liked T.D.'s style, felt they could identify with it, much more so than with the rituals and paraphernalia of the fancy dowsers.

"Dowsing is simple," T.D. would say. "Don't muck it up, don't complicate it. Dowse everywhere, in lush, green, happy fields and in barren, sad fields. Folks think you find good stuff only in beautiful places or only in sad places; you can find water—good, sparkling, refreshing water—everywhere."

T.D. wasn't sure how the dowsing thing worked. He made no claim to any special powers, spiritual insight or mystical ability. It was just something he could do. He could find water in the most likely, expected places and in the most unlikely, unexpected places. As he often said, "I just find good stuff hidden in ordinary places."

In his seventies, T.D. spent his time occasionally dowsing for water but mostly teaching the people of Lanesville the fine art of dowsing—dowsing as T.D. in his old age understood it. He told the people in Lanesville that dowsing is much more than walking around with a branched twig trying to find something in the ground. Dowsing for T.D. was the ability to always find the extraordinary hidden in the ordinary.

He reminded the people of Lanesville that they could all dowse. He said dowsing was "not that special." He told them they had all the dowsing equipment they would ever need, had it with them all the time—their eyes, ears, taste, nose, touch and feelings.

He taught the people of Lanesville that all the people, places and events that made up their lives were the fields in which they were to dowse and in which they could find numerous hidden treasures. "Just find good stuff hidden in all those ordinary places," he told them over and over.

Although he died several years ago, T.D. lives on in Lanesville. For at each wedding ceremony, each funeral oration, each high school graduation, each move to a new job or new house, people all join in with the words, "Thar she blows!"

The *Lanesville Gazette* doesn't have obituaries or birth announcements or even a current events column. All it has is a feature entitled, "Thar She Blows." For the citizens of Lanesville—taught so well by T.D.—know that each current event, each birth and each death is a potential gusher containing the extraordinary in the ordinary.

Winning and Losing

Jacob-like I wrestle with your death
   Sometimes I'm on top winning
   Sometimes your death wins.

When I'm winning
   your death is a new life
      a new start
         for me
         for you.

When I'm winning
   the separation between life and death
      here and there
      falls away
Life, death, here, there, merge into now
   and we are together.

When I'm winning
   your death is what's meant to be
   the Father's will, pleasure and plan
   occasion for joy
      and shout of triumph.

But when your death is winning
black confusion enters the night
frustration at where are you
despair at how are you
fear at how I will get by.

When your death is winning
the empty house follows me everywhere
wedding rings on dresser haunt
smiling grey haired couples anger me.

Seeing

Hank Burrows leaned carefully over the pool table eyeing the eight ball. He wanted to bank it off the side rail into the opposite side pocket. He arched his body parallel to the table, judging distance and force. He knew he was a good pool player— "Shark," others called him. His only weakness was his eyesight— things far away sometimes became blurred. He wanted to make this shot, not just to retain his reputation or pocket the $20 bet he had with Johnny Kuhns, but especially to impress shapely, skinny, long-legged Pattie Carson, who was watching the game.

Both he and Pattie were seventeen and at seventeen showing off is an activity of daily living.

Hank arched again over the table, slowly drew the pool stick back and shot. He missed. As soon as he shot he knew he had missed. The ball was too far away. He couldn't get it in focus. Johnny laughed, picked up the $20 and left the pool hall with Pattie.

Hank walked out of the poolroom slowly. He was depressed, he wasn't used to losing at pool. He was also concerned about his eyesight. He could see fine when looking at things close to him, but the farther away things were the harder it was to see them. It was getting worse week by week. At a distance trees, cars, street signs and even girls were becoming a blur.

When he got home, Hank had to tell his mother about the

pool game. He was broke and needed to borrow money. She knew he had $20 when he left the house and refused to lend him money until he told her what happened to it.

So he described his embarrassing loss, describing in detail his difficulty in seeing the eight ball even though it was just a few feet away from him. For good measure, to create sympathy and grease the way for the loan, he also told his mother how hard it was to see the blackboard at school from his back row seat.

Three days later Hank found himself in an optometrist's office being fitted for a pair of glasses. His mother had made the appointment for him, insisted that he keep it and now demanded, with the optometrist, that he start wearing glasses.

The doctor told him, "You have myopia. That's a fancy name for an eye condition in which visual images come to focus in front of your retina. Myopia is a condition in the eye resulting in defective vision of distant objects. Things close to you, you see fine; those far away are hard to see."

"These will help," the doctor said as he fitted Hank with glasses.

For a seventeen-year-old jock like Hank, glasses are worse than acne. Hank hated them. He associated the glasses with everything he didn't want to be—nerd, four-eyes, bookworm, weakling. He couldn't imagine going out with the gang in glasses; what would girls think?

The first few hours of school in glasses were as bad as Hank thought they would be. Friends and strangers had a good time at his expense—offering to hold his hand to help him up the stairs, inquiring about his seeing-eye dog. The barbs were good-natured and bothered Hank some, but he was more concerned about wearing glasses than he was about the ribbing. What would the glasses do to his various sports activities? Would he still be able to crawl under cars replacing damaged transmissions, oil pans and gears?

Most of all, he worried what the glasses would do to his social life. Would he still be attractive to girls, would peers be uncomfortable around him? The glasses made him sad, anxious and apprehensive. He felt as if one life had ended and a new one started.

There was a video on current events in social studies. Hank took his place in his usual back row seat, expecting to watch the usual confused, jumbled mass of figures and colors move across the blurred, unfocused screen that he had grown used to. To his surprise, sharp, clear, distinct figures made their appearance.

Hank was stunned. Before the glasses, people flashed by him on the screen as a mass of unfocused humanity—lifeless, emotionless, faceless. Now with the glasses, he could see their every emotion, every desperate breath, every twitch and movement.

The same thing happened to him at church the following Sunday. His usual activity during Mass was to gaze around blurry-eyed at the indistinct crowd in church with him. With the glasses on, however, he could see clearly: old Mr. Jacob, tearstained from his wife's death two months ago; Joe and Harriet Simpson, tight-lipped as their marriage rapidly deteriorated towards divorce; Tim Pierce, out of a job for three months, holding his small daughter in his arms; the Millers, hugging their Down Syndrome infant closely; Mike Buckley and Susan Artz, anxiously looking forward to their wedding three weeks away.

Seeing clearly with his glasses, Hank was able to feel close to them. The glasses opened new doors for him, led him to see the hurt, pain, joy and happiness of others.

Hank found himself offering a small prayer of thanks for the uncomfortable, pinching object on his face. He still didn't want the glasses, would never have asked or prayed for them, but at least he could be grateful for the expanded vision they gave him. This new vision was a partial answer to his adolescent, "Why? Why do I have to have these glasses? Why did this happen to me?"

Daisy

The daisies are blooming,
   how you loved them.
I had it made
A bunch of daisies
   for birthday
      anniversary
         "I'm sorry" days
Got me pretty much what I wanted.

These birthdays, anniversaries, "I'm sorry" days
   now wave in the daisy patch.
In the daisies I see
   a life
   a relationship
   a love
I see the mystery of me and you.

So riot, daisy, riot
   bring a tear to my eye
Dance, daisy, dance
   bring a smile to my step
Sing, daisy, sing
   of the one who loved me, too.

The Back Door

Once upon a time, a long time ago, in a land far, far away, there lived a king named Herman. King Herman was a most kind and generous person—a king who wanted the very best for all his subjects. He especially liked to have his citizens come visit him in the palace. There he would talk with them, learn their problems and concerns, and try to find ways to make their lives better. He often kept them for days in the palace. The King's ultimate plan was to have the citizens live full-time with him.

The king, however, had one problem—his citizens were poor, rustic, most unsophisticated. Whenever they came to visit him, they were overwhelmed. The splendor of the palace, the majesty of the king, the trappings of royalty, were all too much for them. King Herman wanted his subjects to feel at home in the palace surroundings, but they couldn't do it. Their normal, usual lives were so barren, so sterile and dull, that the palace and the king left them uncomfortable, practically speechless and most ill-at-ease.

To remedy this, the king decided to put a back door in the palace. He arranged it so that people would enter through a back door, then make their way through the palace and then, after going through several rooms, each progressively more splendid and elegant, come into the throne room and visit with the king. Entering the back door and going through the palace was designed to prepare citizens gradually for entrance into the throne room and eventually have them become so comfortable with palace surroundings that they could live there permanently.

The back door was placed in the palace and citizens used it, but with little success. Oh, they were better prepared by going through the several rooms, but it wasn't enough. It became evident that they needed more preparation, for their lives were truly desolate.

So the king extended the back door concept and put a large garden in back of the palace. Citizens coming to see him were to go through the garden, then through the back door of the palace, then through the several progressively more elegant rooms and then finally come into the presence of the king.

To aid the preparation process, the king placed in the garden all kinds of wonderful things: trees ripe with a wide variety of fruits; bushes that gave off magnificent scents; birds of all kinds with varied plumage. In the garden were all kinds of animals: lions, tigers, bears, dogs, cats, snakes, even a replica of Noah's Ark. All these were designed to prepare citizens for the grandeur of palace living.

The king also saw to it that the garden had a variety of weather. As the citizens went through one section, the sun was shining but there was a cool breeze. Another section had hot, humid weather; another snow. And the wind blew furiously in another section, creating tornados and hurricanes.

Finally, set up along the paths in the garden were small booths where the citizens could obtain a large variety of food and drink: rich, savory beef; sour and sweet wines; sparkling waters; luscious red and orange melons; food and drink the citizens never had in their usual, sterile lives. As they sampled these foods on their way to the palace through the back door garden, they were being prepared, slowly and gradually, for palace life.

It now took citizens a rather long time to get through the garden and then the back door and the progressively more elegant rooms and into the throne room to see the king. But now with the back door arrangements they were much better prepared to see the king and talk with him—and much better prepared for one day living with the king.

Yet some people were found still unprepared for their visit with the king, for they had rushed through the garden not seeing, not hearing, not smelling as they passed the garden's many wonders. Even when they reached the progressively more elegant rooms leading to the throne room, many just walked through, sensing little or nothing, not seeing the magnificence, wonder and beauty as back doors to the throne room.

The king tried to solve this by placing members of his court along the paths of the garden and in the progressively more elegant rooms. His staff would point out to people going through the garden and rooms the various items which would prepare them for the king. They even took people by the hand and walked with them, doing all they could to make sure the citizens were prepared.

Over the years the king added more and more back doors to the palace. In fact, the whole kingdom became a series of back doors, with every facet of life becoming a back door to someplace else.

And, thus, everyone did end up living happily ever after in the palace, for the palace encompassed the entire kingdom.

The Then of Now

The other day I passed one of the several houses
    in which we lived together
Thoughts tumbled, images flashed.

How much of our future we planned in that house
    retirement
    school for kids
    better house
    back to school for you
    insurance
    old age together.

That house was our future
    too bad it wasn't our then now
        the then now of how you felt
        the then now of us
        the then now of who we were
            how deep, broad our relationship
            how wide, expressive our love.

That house was the then of tomorrow
    instead of the then of now.

Conflagration

It was an ordinary church, not architecturally significant—just a simple, cinder block building, originally designed to be a parish social hall. Then, as the number of parishioners declined and building costs escalated, all plans for building a "real" church disappeared and the cinder block social hall became the real church.

All of this made little difference to Peter Hummel. The cinder block building, whatever its original design and purpose, was where he found God, so to him it was a real church. In this building he and Kay were married, here his children were baptized, here he confessed his sinfulness, here each week he was united with his God.

In this building, especially in late afternoon when shadows lengthened, casting the interior of the building in a soft, dim light, Peter would kneel or sit in a word-less, image-less silence, paying attention to God while God paid attention to him. This place was special for Peter, it exuded the sacred, the holy, the other. Friends he knew had other sacred places—woods, streams, mountains—but this very human structure was Peter's sacred place.

Then the cinder-block-social-hall-become-church caught on fire and burned to the ground. The newspaper called it not a fire but a conflagration, for the building and all it contained were totally destroyed. Usually church fires scorch walls, maybe weaken the foundation or destroy statues. This fire, however, burned with such fury and intensity that nothing was left. "Burned to the ground" was an understatement.

While all the parishioners were upset by the loss of the church, Peter was devastated. The rest lost their place of worship, their place of social gathering. Peter, though, lost his God. Gone was the place he daily found God, gone was the place of union... of communion. Gone even was Peter's peace of mind for he felt that God could somehow have prevented the fire.

"God is supposed to be omnipotent," Peter thought. "If He is omnipotent, then He can do anything." Peter tried to reconcile the omnipotence of God with the destruction of his sacred space, but he couldn't. If God is all-powerful, why didn't He repair the church's wiring? Such a simple act for One all-powerful. Or was it that God is indifferent—all-powerful but aloof from the real, practical world of Peter? Peter's mind spun as he tried to reconcile his loss with the power and goodness of God he had been taught about all his life.

Peter found that his God died when the church burned. The God of his youth faded away and smoldered in the ashes of the destroyed sacred place. In the months after his loss, Peter buried his old God and found a new One. Peter's new God was still omnipotent, still good, but His power and goodness encompassed the paradox of destruction and weakness. Peter slowly discovered a new presence of God, now not localized, not limited to a particular place or space.

Peter often returns to the corner of Fourth and Hickory streets and visits the charred remains of the cinder block church. He would like to have it back, but knows the scorched remains will never be a church again.

Several of his friends have suggested to Peter that he find another church in which to seek God, but he always says, "No. Not now. Not yet anyway." He knows another church would provide him with physical and emotional comfort, would give him joy when afternoon shadows lengthen. But no. Not yet anyway.

Remember Me

Your greatest fear
    was being forgotten.
So often
    especially in the last days
You wondered aloud,
"Will you, will they, remember me?"

You are remembered
    in home arrangements and decorations
    in speech, walk, mannerisms of children
    in temptations to stray
    in prayers and Masses.

Yet your fear was justified
    for remembering is not automatic
We have to work at it
    for memories do fade.

°It seems Jesus had this fear, too.
"Do this in memory of me," and
"When the Paraclete comes
    He will remind you of all I said."

The Giraffe

In Africa many eons ago there lived a giraffe. In fact, there were many giraffes in Africa, but this particular giraffe, whom everyone called Jerry, was special. Jerry was very curious. He was always poking around in things—the ground, or trees or bushes—trying to discover all he could.

At this time in the evolution of giraffes, they didn't have long necks. Their necks were much like the necks of horses or zebras. It was curious Jerry who started the giraffes on their way to long necks.

You see, while the other giraffes were eating leaves from a tree or from a bush, while they poked around in the ground grubbing for small, tender shoots, all they did was eat. But not Jerry. While eating, he was constantly stretching out his neck, leaning forward, straining to see what was behind a leaf or under and around the grass.

Jerry drove the other giraffes crazy as they stood waiting their turn to eat. They would often shout at him, "Jerry, hurry up and eat. Stop the looking. We could starve standing here waiting for you."

But Jerry never hurried. Slowly, gently, quietly, he studied each leaf, each bush, each root, asking, "Why is it green?" or "Where did this come from?"

As he reached to see behind and beyond his world, Jerry would often sense a presence. He felt someone was there—hiding, laughing, loving—behind each thing he encountered. This presence, this there-ness, was vague, indistinct, elusive, but so enticing to Jerry. For the presence would explain so much: the color and shape of the leaf, the texture of the root, the nourishment of the bush; the how, why and what of so many things in his world. The more Jerry sensed this presence, the more he stretched for it, and the longer his neck grew.

Sometimes Jerry would try to rush his eating or hurry his looking, but he just couldn't. The discovery of the presence that was behind and beyond was too overpowering. It was like a hand in him fitting into an old, familiar glove. The presence was calm, quiet, familiar. So Jerry nibbled, never gobbled, savoring each morsel.

When Jerry's wife died, the giraffes watched him closely. "Wonder how he will chew on that?" they asked. Like to everything else, Jerry stretched out to his wife's death, asking the "Why?" and "Who?" and "What?" questions. As he chewed on the death twig he was tempted to spit it out—its bitterness soured his stomach. Often the thought crossed his mind, "There's nothing in this twig. It's nothing but a twig." In time, with repeated looking, searching and quiet reflection, however, Jerry eventually found the same presence he discovered everywhere else—even in the harsh, bitter fact of his wife's death.

Over time, other giraffes joined Jerry in his stretching, in his reaching out, in his looking behind and beyond. These, too, started growing long necks, and the long-neck giraffes huddled together, intermarried and eventually were the only ones to survive. You see, the giraffes who refused to look behind and beyond, who refused to stretch and reach out, who offhandedly rejected the bitter-tasting, simply died off. They starved to death eating the easy and refusing to seek nourishment from the difficult.

Ultimate Love

Death creates ultimate love
    lifts love up way beyond senses
    for there is nothing
        no body
        no touch
        no laugh
        nothing
But you.

You dead
    touch nothing but my spirit.
You dead
    I touch nothing but your spirit.

The Weight Lifter

Little eight-year-old Harry Edgeworth was building sand castles. He was vacationing in Hawaii with his parents and was having a wonderful, creative time with the clean, white sand of Waikiki.

As Harry finished his castle, down the beach came Jack Smothers, who was a bully. Jack was about five years older than Harry and was built about six times bigger. When Jack saw the sand castle, replete with towers, moat and drawbridge, he headed straight for it, shouting and kicking sand. Then Jack ran through the castle complex, totally destroying it.

Harry sat in the sand. His first instinct was to go after Jack and rip him apart. But Harry was a realist. He knew a fight with Jack would be useless. Jack was too big. Jack would just demolish him like he demolished the castle. Harry sat quietly in the sand, feeling the anger, frustration, indignation, injustice and helplessness that comes from experiencing a situation over which no control is possible.

Harry was stunned. He had worked so long and so hard to get the castle complex just how he wanted it. Now it was gone. Its going was so swift. It was there; then seconds later it was gone.

Harry gathered up his shovels, his bucket and his spoons and retreated to the safety of his parents' blanket, thinking perhaps he could forget about the castle, pretend it never happened. Such denial, of course, was unrealistic, but Harry, in his shock and sorrow, reached out for any thought that offered some solace or security.

When the Edgeworths finished their vacation in Hawaii and returned to Chicago, Harry had nightmares about Jack Smothers and the destruction of his castle. Try as he might he could not forget about what had occurred on the beach. His anger and pain ate away at him.

Even at his young age, Harry realized he couldn't just sit and feel sorry for himself. He had to do something to help him give meaning to this experience of loss.

There were many things, Harry realized, that he could do to help himself get over the destruction of his castle, but weight lifting was the thing that appealed to him. Learning to lift things up, he thought, would give him the muscle he seemed to lack. So Harry Edgeworth became a weight lifter.

He had his parents buy him some dumbbells and a machine, called a Universal Gym; they bought small weights for his wrists and ankles and a set of big iron weights with a bar with which to lift them.

Then Harry practiced—bench presses, leg stretches, cling and snatch. Every day, several times a day, Harry was lifting, pulling, stretching, bending.

Every day his muscles grew. Christmas, Easter, birthdays—all Harry wanted for presents were new weights, a new bench, new springs.

As he lifted, Harry knew he had chosen the right activity to get him over the pain of the Hawaii experience—the feeling of helplessness he felt when he could not protect himself and his castle.

When Harry lifted, he lifted more than the weights. As the bar rose over his head he thought of Jack Smothers. As he threw the bar and its weights to the floor he aimed them at the bully. As his muscles rippled he knew he could handle anybody. No longer was Harry a fifty-pound weakling needing to retreat to the safety of his parents' blanket.

When Harry graduated from middle school he was really big and strong. Nobody dared mess with any of Harry's "castles."

Harry lifted his way through high school, became an all-state lifter. College was the same. You name it, Harry lifted it—higher, quicker and longer than anyone in the country. He went on to the Olympics, the one in Barcelona in '92, and won several weight lifting medals. Harry Edgeworth had become a great weight lifter.

Throughout his lifetime of lifting, Harry never forgot Jack Smothers. Because of Jack he started lifting. Jack in a perverse way made Harry a weight lifter. Jack didn't build Harry's muscles—Harry did that for himself. But Jack did provide the occasion for Harry to make himself strong and powerful, and for that Harry thanked him.

Your Now Touch

I need you a thousand times a day
    does this tie match?
    how long to cook the noodles?
    how best support the kids?

And I try to remember
what you said
    what you did
        and how.

How you were present
    to house things
    to kid stuff.

What you liked
    in food
    in furniture
    in Easter and Christmas decorations.

My memories of you
    are your now touch.

The Strange Dad

Six-year-old Leon Christian was having trouble with his dad. His father was nice to him, played ball with him, took care of him in every way, but—from Leon's point of view—his dad was strange. Leon hesitated to use the word "weird," but at times he did think his dad was weird.

For instance, his dad ate unfrosted Shredded Wheat for breakfast. His dad could have whatever he wanted for breakfast— Boo Berries, Count Chocula, or even Frosted Flakes—but he chose Shredded Wheat. That was weird, Leon thought.

When Leon made the suggestion that he, his dad and his mom sleep together, his dad turned him down. Leon knew they were a family, knew that they all liked each other and always had a lot of fun around bedtime. So, why not sleep together? But his dad said, "No way."

"Weird," thought Leon.

When the family dog, Ursula, died, Leon was devastated. He had a very hard time with her death and he missed her very much. She had been a part of the family since his birth. His dad, however, while sad, did not appear to Leon to be devastated by the death. It was weird, like he knew something Leon didn't know.

There were so many other things Leon didn't understand

about his father. His dad took a shower every day, even though nobody made him do it. His dad had plenty of money in his pocket, enough to buy bags and bags of candy for himself, but he never did. His dad could stay up at night as late as he wanted to, yet was in bed most nights by 10:30. And his dad watched the news on T.V. instead of cartoons!

When Leon looked around his six-year-old world, he saw he was not alone. Tommy, June, Helen, Mark and Andy had the same concerns about their dads. "Why can't I have a motor scooter?" or "Why won't he buy me the latest heavy metal tape?" or "Why does he go to work every day?" floated through and filled the world of his friends. Everyone's dad, it seemed, was a strange person, doing what no six-year-old would ever do and not doing what any sensible six-year-old would do.

For months, Leon struggled with the idea that his dad was weird. He tried to understand his dad, tried to figure him out. As his dad continued to do weird things, however, Leon just gave up.

When he thought about it, Leon knew that "giving up on his dad" was not exactly what he was doing. Rather he was recognizing a reality—or perhaps reconciling several realities. His father's love was real, but some of his father's actions were hard to understand as being part of this love. So Leon in effect decided to give his father the benefit of the doubt. Leon just decided to trust his father's goodness.

He concluded that the ways of a dad were not the ways of a six-year-old. He began to realize that his dad was totally, completely different from a six-year-old. So Leon gave up trying to understand his dad. He let his dad be a dad.

Still, Leon pauses once in a while as thoughts of "weird dad" float through his head. Letting a dad be a dad is not a once and done decision. It has to be repeated over and over as part of the never-ending relationship between father and son.

How Do I Miss You?

How do I miss you
    let me count the ways.

I miss you in a clean house
    my clean is just clean
    yours was smelly, frilly clean.

I miss you in a bed too large
    in covers no longer pulled away from me.

I miss you in the empty car seat next to me
    in silence when I exceed the speed limit.

I miss you in buttons falling off my jacket
    in wrong size shirts I just bought.

How do I miss you?
    I miss you in fleshy,
    daily,
    touchable life.

Déjà Vu Orange Juice

In the Center City mall, a few miles south of Orlando, Florida, there was an Orange Julius store. It served the best orange juice on the East coast. The reason it has the best orange juice was Albert Johnson, the former owner of the store. Al just loved to squeeze oranges. He took an orange in his hand and squeezed and squeezed until he got every drop of juice out of it. Most of the time he didn't even bother to peel the orange. The rind, the pulp, the seeds, everything got squeezed and became orange juice. "Most folks are too damn finicky," Al said. "They want the orange peeled, seeded, all nice and clean. You get good juice when you squeeze the whole thing, just as it is."

We walked these streets together, seldom holding hands. What a shame! Each of us wrapped in private thoughts, plans and other silly life stuff. I walk these streets with you now, reach out with you and grab the stores, the houses, the trees, the people, the very air, and with you squeeze out their all.

Al had several machines in the store—large, gleaming, stainless steel machines which spun the oranges around and around and extracted their juice.

Al, though, liked to hand-squeeze the oranges. He said his hand got more juice out of the oranges than any machine ever could. He believed you had to get personally involved in the squeezing. "Nobody, no thing, no machine can do the squeezing for you," he always contended.

How often we squeezed sex until it became love, the last drops of afterglow binding us tightly together. We missed a lot, but got most of it, didn't we?

One summer, between college semesters, I worked for Al in his Orange Julius place. What a trip! He was a fanatic about oranges and their juice. He knew all the varieties of oranges— which ones had thick skin, which thin; which were seedless, which loaded with seeds; which ones had slices that separated easily. He told me all about oranges. He explained the sad shriveled ones, the plump jolly ones, the thin-skinned intellectual ones, the ones with sour juice that pucker your lips and bring tears to your eyes. He would get all excited as he talked about sweet, sensuous oranges whose juice ran down your chin and made your lips smack. He could talk for hours about oranges that were to be shared and those to be hugged to yourself, about party oranges and solitary oranges, holiday oranges and Lenten oranges. He could go on and on about oranges that filled you up and oranges that left you hungry. Al knew all there was to know about oranges. "Got to," he used to say. "The more you know about oranges, the more you know about squeezing them—how hard, how long, which fingers to use. The more you know, the better you squeeze. The better you squeeze, the better the juice."

Both of us had honest religious feelings. Yet we often prayed as two, seldom as one. Our religion was mostly "me-and-God," when it should have been "we-and-God." We now pray together always. Death creates unity in our prayer. Now I spend time in church with you, in fact I am with you all the time. The separation of death paradoxically brings many things together.

The summer I worked with Al, I got to know him very well. I learned how he got his orange squeezing ability: Al squeezed everything. He got the last drop out of everything he did. Take the way he played golf! He ran around the course, hooking, slicing, three-and-four putting greens, laughing, swinging, enjoying all eighteen holes. Golf for Al was just an occasion to squeeze life. He cared little about par, bogey, or breaking a hundred. Just so the golf course and everyone around it was wrung dry when he finished.

How many nights, weekends, we spent watching TV, silently. We weren't angry, we weren't bored with each other. Maybe we just weren't trying hard enough to explore our depths, plumb the what, how and why of our relationship. Since your death, we relate deeply. Maybe missing, not having but wanting, creates a special kind of relationship.

It was exhausting watching Al move through life. His car was the sleekest, fastest available. He gobbled food on the run and savored it in all-night suppers. His clothes never matched. Money for him was just a ticket to get into life's various rooms and there give life a good shake. Driving, drinking, eating, jogging were singular events for Al, never occasions for something else.

Your job, my job, this meeting, that volunteering! We had, or maybe we took, too little "we-time." I don't regret this. We had other responsibilities, many talents to share. I have changed however. I now make time for just the two of us.

Al, despite his hectic life, was a very religious person. Often he would pray all day. Starting early in the morning, he continued until late at night. His prayer was not the usual stuff, a set of formalized, verbal prayers. Rather, Al sat and paid attention to what he called the "Loving Presence." Prayer for him was where he got the energy he used to squeeze his various oranges. He was the only person I knew who sweated while he prayed.

What a match we made! How did we ever get together? A saver and a spender. A "There's no tomorrow" and a "There's always a rainy tomorrow. " You always won, of course, and you were right. We lived supporting mortgage companies, GMAC were our middle initials. Sears, Kaufmann's, Montgomery Ward all loved us and our charge cards. But we got every drop of juice out of our lives together.

What I especially liked about Al was his hope, his optimism. For him there was always another orange out there to squeeze. Maybe on a given day when he was tired or in a hurry he would leave a lot of juice in one orange. But he always reached for the next one and enthusiastically squeezed it. Each time was a new chance to get out all the juice. As he said, "Keep squeezing 'til you get it right." Al always dealt with the orange in his hand, the "here and now" orange—not the one before or the one to come. He knew that, while there was always another orange out there, the one in his hand would never be there again.

Even in the last days, even when we knew they were the last days, we never discussed death. Not like we do now. Maybe death is one of those things you just can't discuss when you have no experience of it.

Perhaps you've noticed that many Orange Julius stores never become successful, successful anyway like Al's place. One of the reasons is they don't get the last drop of juice from each orange. You see, to get really good orange juice you've got to squeeze until you get into the juice the sun that warmed the orange, the rain and wind that helped it grow. You've got to squeeze until you get into the juice the richness of the orange grove soil, the sweat of the farm workers. You've got to squeeze until you extract that "Loving Presence" which lies deep in every orange. Really good orange juice is *déjà vu* orange juice.

I wake up in the middle of the night sensing that something is terribly wrong. Then I realize what is wrong. You are dead.

In ten seconds, in the pit of my stomach, I relive three years of cancer, one week of dying, one day of viewing, two hours of burial. All feeling leaves my body except that wave of nausea in my stomach. But I am beginning to see that life is not over. You are not over, I am not over, we are not over. With each passing day I know there are too many oranges out there for us to be finished.

Al retired last year and sold his orange juice store to me. It was the best buy I ever made. For squeezing oranges, getting all the juice, is more than a business. It's a lifestyle—a lifestyle that proves you can go around more than once. You can go around with each orange you squeeze.

The Lover

It's difficult to imagine that Someone
    could love you more than I,
    want you more than I

But if you were a gift
    how great the Giver.

It's hard to accept
    that you more went to Him
        then left me.

But if you were a love,
    what must be the Lover
    if you were a spark,
    what the Fire
    if you were a refracted rainbow,
    what the pure, white Light.

The Whale

In the deep, dark, blue sea, there lived a whale whose name was Wallace. Wallace was the king of the sea. Large. Powerful. Master of the deep, dark, blue sea. Royal and regal.

Once, as Wallace was majestically swimming through his kingdom of the sea, having fun lifting his gigantic tail high in the air and slapping it down on the water with a mighty thud, he saw in the distance another whale.

Seeing another whale was not that unusual for Wallace, but there was something different about this particular whale. Oh, the other whale was large like him. The other whale split the sea in huge, powerful undulations like he did. But the other whale was also dainty. Sleek and attractive. For the other whale was a she and Wallace was a he. In fact, the more Wallace realized the other whale was a she, the more he understood he was a he.

In time, Wallace fell in love with and married this large, powerful, yet dainty, female whale, whose name was Whitney. And Whitney changed his life. Wallace was still master of the sea. Birds and fishes, dolphins and lobsters still scattered as he swam through the water. But with Whitney, Wallace found the sea bluer, the water cooler, the air around his huge body vibrant and alive. When he thought about his wife, he would surge to the surface of the sea, leap high out of the water and spout a huge spray straight up into the sky. Whitney colored his day, warmed his night and flavored his every majestic movement through the sea.

As the years passed, the sea found more whales splitting its waves. Small, tiny whales, three of them—two boys and a girl—the children of Whitney and Wallace.

Wallace found life with his family glorious. Sure, times were often tough. Finding food for Whitney and the three kids was difficult. Teaching the kids the difference between safe, deep water and dangerous shallow water was a constant worry. Finding the right companions for them was always a chore. But Wallace, Whitney and the kids were happy, and they all grew in wisdom and in love.

Then the unthinkable happened. One day as Wallace was making his rounds through the sea, performing his kingly duties of settling various fish disputes, nudging fallen coral back onto the reef and dredging sand bars, he felt a strange vibration in the sea. Violent shocks of water flowed all around him. Waves came running through the water in short, slapping, hurting movements. Wallace became alarmed. He knew Whitney was alone, the three kids were away at school. He headed for home as fast as his splashing tail could carry him. The waves and ripples of water became more turbulent the nearer to home he got.

About a mile from their home, as Wallace raised his head above the water, he saw it. A large, steel, black, whaling boat bobbing on the waves. Whitney was floating upside down behind the boat, harpoons protruding from her sleek, powerful, dainty—and now dead—body.

Dark, black anger flowed through every inch of Wallace's huge frame. He roared high into the air, out of the sea and charged the whaling boat. Again and again he charged, filling the air and the sea with the mist and sound of his slapping tail. But each time he was beaten back by the whalers. How do you fight a mechanized whaling boat? How do you confront an enemy mounted with nets, tongs, spears and large, steel, electronically controlled harpoons? How do you battle death itself? The whaling boat floated up and down on the waves, unconquered and unmoved by Wallace's fury. After many futile charges, Wallace, exhausted and frustrated, slowly swam away, glancing back now and then at the body of Whitney being towed behind the whaling vessel.

Despite his sadness, Wallace quickly gathered his children together. With them and a few friends, he held a brief memorial service for Whitney. Then, choking back his tears, sometimes unsuccessfully, Wallace got about the business of getting on with his life, his life without Whitney. He was, after all, king of the sea. Large. Powerful. Majestic. Master. Whatever the pain, whatever the anger, he had his work to carry on. So he started again to plow the sea-lanes, alone and lonely, performing his duties as king.

As Wallace moved schools of fish into the safety of deeper water, as he splashed the sea with his tail to ward off sharks, as he spouted water into the air testing its purity, he found the sea was no longer blue. It was colorless. The water was neither warm nor cold. It was just there. His kids continued to grow in size, but Wallace was detached from the joy and excitement of their development.

Then one day Wallace realized what was happening to him. He realized he was killing Whitney more effectively than the whalers had. They killed her body, but he was killing, unconsciously, her spirit. He killed her spirit when he swam spirit-less through a sea teeming with life. He killed her spirit as he refused to feel the sea's coolness; killed it as he looked at blue water, white birds and red coral and was color blind. He killed Whitney's spirit as he detached himself from the joy and exuberance of his children's lives.

Wallace finally felt grief—true grief for his true loss. He touched his sadness, for Whitney's death was truly sad. He knew the sorrow as his own, a reality which flowed from the glorious reality of his life with Whitney. Grief, sadness, sorrow were his real feelings, not to be hated or despised—just embraced as his own.

Wallace wept until he was empty, free of his suppressed anger and hurt. He wept until he could say both good-bye to Whitney and then hello to her again. He admitted for the first time that Whitney was really gone. No more pretending. No more make-believe. No more fantasy. No more constant return to the scene of her death. Yet he also knew she would forever color, warm, and flavor his every movement through the sea. Wallace buried Whitney's body and embraced her spirit, feeling it flow through him.

Good-Bye

One cool, early morning
    a hearse came to the door.
They asked me to leave the room
    as your body was removed.

I tried to say good-bye then
    but the death wound
    was too raw to be touched.

I knelt beside your body at the church
    as you were eulogized and funeral-massed.
Then walked out behind you.

I tried to say good-bye then
    but you were too freshly gone
    for me to admit your absence.

Grave site rites designed to say good-bye
    flower-ed
        dirt-ed
            tent-ed
Were much too stark and barren
    for final parting.

Even grave visits
    where we are most alone
Were much too painful
    too necessary
    for good-bye.

Now, with time
    with these rambling writings
    and with the understanding that
    good-bye is not to all of you
        but only body
            only physical presence,

I can say
    "Good-bye,
        Good-bye, my love."